Your Infidel Eyes

Also by Brant Lyon

You Are White Inside
(under the name B. R. Lyon)
New York City: Three Rooms Press, 2011.

gape-seed
Editor with Ice Gayle Johnson, Jane Ormerod, Thomas
    Fucaloro
New York City: Uphook Press, 2011.

hell strung and crooked
Editor with Ice Gayle Johnson, Jane Ormerod, Thomas
    Fucaloro
New York City: Uphook Press, 2010.

you say. say.
Editor with Ice Gayle Johnson, Jane Ormerod
New York City: Uphook Press, 2009.

*A Cautionary Tale: Peer into the Lives of Seven New York
    Performing Poets*
With Theo Coates, Pete Dolack, Bob Hart, Ice Gayle Johnson,
    Jane Ormerod, Frank Simone
New York City: Uphook Press, 2008.

Brant Lyon has given us a ride into his poet's soul. He writes,"Truth / runs to you / with outstretched arms." This is Brant, we feel and hear, welcoming us. Bringing us into exotic or commonplace settings, never holding back a detail, he will even make us smile. Subject matter—people, places, whatever it may be (even toilet paper)—is treated with equal dignity and respect. It deepens us into the *inner* mind. In "Quang Tri" he writes, "There is no asylum for the fugitive past," then brings us back, informed, and safe. In "Telephony" the phone is a conch shell: "It's not the ocean's roar I hear, / but wishful thinking." Yes, and wonderful. Brant mixes the most personal with the spiritual, taking us to faroff shores, as if walking us through the well-lit rooms of a temple of the divine.

—**Evie Ivy**, author of *No, No Nonets . . . the Book of Nonets*

Brant Lyon was an exceptional writer and Brownstone Poet, as well as an artiste, friend, and humanitarian. His genius weighed in megatons. He was the universal sun in search of a world without borders. His poetry danced in the Dakhla, played the I Ching, and needed to be blessed by the Mumbai monsoon. Like Krishna's flute, Brant's words became his legacy: ". . . the bee that pollinates / your dreams."

—**Patricia Carragon**, Curator, Editor-in-Chief, Brownstone Poets

The first time I read *Your Infidel Eyes* was on a crowded A train in New York City, traveling home from Brooklyn to Harlem, after a Saturday night rehearsal with Brant. I was riveted. This second edition is a welcome addition to the libraries of all who dare to live and love in these "interesting times."

—**Robin Small-McCarthy**, Founder and Co-Host of Kairos Poetry Café

Your Infidel Eyes

Brant Lyon

10th ANNIVERSARY EDITION

POETS WEAR PRADA • Hoboken, New Jersey

Your Infidel Eyes

Copyright © 2006, 2016 Brant Lyon

Poets Wear Prada
533 Bloomfield Street, Second Floor
Hoboken, New Jersey 07030
http://pwpbooks.blogspot.com

First North American Publication 2006
Second / Mass Market Paperback Edition 2016

Grateful acknowledgment is made to Patricia Carragon who previously published "I Ching" in *Brownstone Poets Anthology*, 2009.

ISBN-13: 978-0692679333
ISBN-10: 0692679332

Printed in the U.S.A.

Front Cover Photo: Brant Lyon
Author Photo: D. Cloherty

For Frank, who always believed I could.

For Roxanne, who insisted I should.

For Hassan, who taught me to eat with my right hand,
and the good people of Dakhla oasis, Egypt,
who never laughed but cheered me on whenever I danced.

Table of Contents

"Just a little off the top, Joe."

Your Infidel Eyes

ॐ

TRUTH

runs to you
with outstretched arms
always believing
you'll swoop it up in yours
and lift it
high
always believing
it will see itself
reflected in the vacant pupils
of your infidel eyes
always believing
you'll indulge
its selfish unreasonable
annihilating demands
and spoil it rotten
as you would
an adorable child

ILLUSION

You have been my jailer
long enough, and stupid, too!
While you were snoring
slumped in your chair
I angled the keys from
the slackened grip
of your miserable hand
and freed myself,
locking you inside the cell
instead.

I CHING

Emperor Fu Hsi imagined he saw
the marks of yin and yang
on a tortoise shell
and that is when the trouble began.

Fifty yarrow sticks,
sixty-four hexagrams, and
four thousand, seven hundred thirty-eight
years later there are still only
four thousand ninety-six ways
to catalogue pain.

There is the pain
of
Not Knowing,
and of
Knowing.
The pain of Certainty,
and of Uncertainty.
The pain of Doing,
and of
Not Doing.
And the pain
of
Not Not-Doing.

A wounded taxonomy—
finite binomial code of yang and yin:
whole and broken lines
configured in The Book of Change.

Facing south,
a lone table centered in the room.
Facing north,
the sage approaches, and solemnly,
the I Ching is taken from its shelf
and placed upon that ominous plane.

He kowtows,
kowtows,
kowtows once more—
three times in clockwise circles
fifty yarrow sticks are passed

through the smoke of incense as
The Inquiry
is burned into his mind,
emptied of all else.

A single stick, culled by chance
is set aside (passive witness
to what the rest portend).
And then:
the ancient arithmetic begins . . .

HOMESICK

I must return to Mumbai in time for monsoon
The wheels of its juggernaut
will trample the countryside into familiar ruts
ineluctable and merciless
No wonder our blue-skinned god
learned compassion for every living thing. and dead.
The rain here is poison and its own antidote
As pain is to love. and love to pain.
I will drive my taxi double shifts to JFK, dark clouds
gathering in my rearview mirror
An eye on the road. an eye to the sky.

Is that his flute I hear so sweetly playing?

VIJAYA DASHAMI

Each widening arc brings his feet closer, closer to touching the cluster of fruit dangling high on the neem tree. "If I should kick it I'll be the fiercest tiger in the village!" But he has never even seen a tiger, in fact, knows no one who has for many years, though foreign tourists and snooty Indians will come and pay good money in hopes of spotting one in Chitwan's national game preserve, just outside his backyard.

"Careful, Shanta!" a woman with a baby perched on her hip warns. "The bamboo poles are lifting off the ground!" In a few days the swing will be taken down until next year, and the children will cry—surely they will find other joys. Last evening Shanta's younger brothers caught frogs that hopped from the rice paddies in search of crickets while I shot the breeze with his uncle Ram.

"You like my tika?" Shanta smiles. "Then you should have one, too."

"But," I protest, "I'm not Hindu. You're not my elder, and so can't bless me, besides."

"You're American," Shanta says. "For you I bend the rules." He asks the name of my profession then recites a prayer. Mixes scarlet powder with sandal-wood paste and grains of rice; presses a glob onto my forehead, then tucks a few blades of sprouted barley behind my ear to augur my good fortune.

⋙ ❀ ⋘

I can't wait to show off my tika to Ram, and to wish him a happy Vijaya Dashami. "How's business?" I inquire.

"The deutsche mark and the dollar are strong, but in my shop sales are slow today; everyone's at home with their families chillin' for the holiday. Nice tika." Ram owns a grocery store and runs an official money exchange for Nepal

Rasta Bank—a wordly, comparatively well-off man who once spent three months in Tokyo.

"This morning I saw two rhinos charge across the river and trample a dugout canoe."

"That's too bad," Ram says, "a lot of hard work goes into making one of those. Imagine: in Japan stressed-out execs will shell out a hundred bucks an hour to sit in some room and meditate as scenes from nature are projected on a screen—don't that beat all!"

"That's hard to top," I sigh, "but let's see . . . In America supermarket shelves overflow with at least a dozen different brands of toilet tissue—each that much more squeezably soft, with chubby, rosy-cheeked babies on their labels, in pink, in blue, or floral designs, scented or non-, 3-ply, quilted as though a goose down comforter, hypo-allergenic if you prefer, 4 or 6 (even more!) rolls shrink-wrapped in econo-paks. In America a man's home is his castle, and all men are kings. As a man sits upon the throne a wave of his hand unspools T. P. in plentiful folds, like thick wads of cash, to wipe his royal ass."

Vijaya Dashami   Hindi: 'The Tenth Day of Victory'; an important Hindu celebration to mark the triumph of Lord Rama over Demon king Ravana

QUANG TRI

For Frank Simone

Even as you lie in a hospital bed
and Intensive Cardiac Care polygraphs waver overhead,
you still soldier on
and open your sketchbook to a blank page,
clear your head

    (it was not for you to bring back all your men)

and steady your hand

    (it was long ago you last held a gun)

to draw the image that lately always comes to mind:

    not grenades but pomegranates.

Bold deployment of colored pens
cover them with psychedelic camouflage.
You depict each pomegranate pulsating whole,
though sometimes misshapen, not one
sliced open to reveal its cache of a thousand rubies—
the light of jewels refracted rather through
the scar left where the rind was plucked from its stem.
Yet each one a radiant wound to learn from.

    It's your heart you're drawing, I said.

And all the while you've been gaining knowledge.
There is no asylum for the fugitive past.
When for the last time on a belly crawl
you rub your nose in it to teach yourself that final lesson

    (you haven't forgotten
      the burning temples of Cambodia, have you?)

and decide not to die but hedge your bets instead
light two candles: one for God, the other for the Devil,
then call upon them both to be your witness:

    douse your karma with gasoline, stand back,
      and toss a match.

TECATE, AFTERNOON

The day comes freighted with its aspirations without a depot.
The way a hornet butts its head against the plate glass,
tantalized by freedom.
We're no different from them—
Muchachos milling about the plaza, truanting.
An old man on a bench dozing in the sun.
That greasy drunk who flails his arms, cursing everybody.
Any *mujer* yelling at her ornery brat
to come back outside the *dulcería*.

No different, really.

TELEPHONY

Your words, a gentle undertow,
could sweep me back out to sea.
Each syllable murmurs, suspires,
then crashes onto shore, and is beached there.

I'm calling all the way from Playa Coyote—
how's our connection?

The phone, a conch shell held ringing in the ear.
It's not the ocean's roar I hear,
but wishful thinking.

THE PECKING ORDER
ON SHARIA AS-SOUQ, ASWAN

At dusk, when the market simmers down,
then cools—a pot brought back to boil by noon
next day—what won't be thrown into that pot
is tossed onto a heap in the middle of Sharia as-Souq
that nightly grows then disappears:

Bone and gristle from the butcher shop,
soggy mint leaves from the corner café,
a crate of tomatoes trampled by a donkey cart,
rotten lemons not even the careless
or desperate would buy . . .

Donkeys lower their muzzles into the pile
and are led away; sheep and goats, a few stray
dogs and cats pick over the trash and take their fill;
next ducks, chickens, and geese furiously peck.

Finally, the mound is set on fire.
Flames feed, in turn, licking air.

SMOKE DREAM

Nessham blows off
the charcoal's feathery ash
and fire rekindles in his eyes.
Black down on his upper lip
wispy as the smoke.
He sits cross-legged and barefoot
hunched over the brazier,
another pellet pinched
between his fingers.
Beautiful. Dutiful.
He tamps tobacco into
the clay bowl that nests the dream.
Far away. Here.
Then tends the embers placed on top.
The nargile passes from
Sayyed to Nasser,
onto Hassan, then me.
Hashish, Nessham hisses
with a winsome smile.
My cock stiffens hard as the needle
dropped onto my lap.
Dorak (it's your turn), reminds my lover
beside me, knee nudging knee.
I don't wipe his spittle off the tip.
Minower, Nessham says.
Inta minower, I reply, expelling the cloud
sucked deep down into my chest.
The night will claim me till dawn.
But I am taken otherwise, so must
refuse what isn't rightly mine.

_____

    minower   Arabic: 'you bring in the light'
    inta minower 'it's you who brings in the light'

LAST LOOK AROUND

Shut the door behind
you but first take
one last look around.
Make your mind
a photographic plate.
Inhale its ghost; each place
has its peculiar scent,
like lion's piss, that leaves
its territorial mark.
Each place absent
its owner, becoming nowhere,
is its true domain.
No use going over
touching things, it's not
your fingertips that must
remember them.
Things must remain as they are.
Their future has already
become their history, turning
over pages in a book
to read what it might have
said before it's written.
The things that don't aren't
the same things as these, so don't
turn your back believing
you've got two of everything.
The one you have, don't have,
is neither.

A LITTLE OFF THE TOP

Joe's Barber Shop isn't closed on Mondays
anymore—it's open for business seven days a week.
And the barber's name isn't Joe—it's now Serge,
from some ex-soviet bloc republic.
With the reliability of the neighborhood mortician
gently there at the time of need, and the bold assurance
of a God who has counted every last one
on a man's head, he cuts hair day in day out
in this great land of freedom and democracy,
because hair will grow for any man until the day
he dies, and then, even for a little while after that.
Besides, he needs the money.
He stands behind a standard-issue pneumatic chair
wearing his green apparatchik smock,
and with his official clippers and scissors in hand,
sees equal opportunity atop every head.
He goes to work shearing off locks, shaving heads,
trimming beards, and—*godblessamerica*—clips
the nose hairs of the old man with more fuzz
on his earlobes than on his pate.
He has spied Serge's shop and come in from the cold.
As though a refugee stumbling on his last legs,
he seeks the asylum of Serge's chair, plunks
down in it, frowning in the mirror like it's some
persecution killing him, and grumbles,
Just a little off the top, Joe.
Serge has nothing to lose, and doesn't correct him.
He minds his business and just snips and grins.

AN OUTLAW SURA

Mine is not a book free
of doubt and involution.
The path I've followed
has not been straight
though I have fulfilled
as best I could
my devotional obligations;
spent what has been given me
toward the charity
of my choosing,
freely levied my own *jaziyah*.
I will remain an infidel,
though in the end
I have not denied
but been led astray
obeying the forbidden
dictates of my heart,
still believing
(what has been revealed)
in the Unknown.
In the name of ever-merciful Love
I have come to cherish love's
most benevolent blasphemies.

_____

sura   Arabic: a chapter of the Qur'an
jaziyah   a tax imposed on non-Muslims for protection and other
   services

TESTIMONY

You've been bruised.
You've been beaten.
You've been there and back.
Been high and low
and felt like hope
three days without water.
Still you raise your hand,
open palm, to testify
what you believe.

You've been sleeping
with the window open.

Now you've been stung.
Your mound of Venus throbs
with an itch no balm can soothe
and wakes you from a fitful sleep.
But your thumb and finger
are too clumsy to remove
its tiny stinger from your hand.

. . . the bee that pollinates
your dreams.

ॐ

A NOTE ABOUT THE TYPE

Beatrice Warde (1900–1969), typography scholar and educator, author of the classic *The Crystal Goblet* (World, 1956), a collection of 16 essays on the subject of book typography, often said the reader's eye should focus "*through* type and not *upon* it." In an address delivered to British Typographers Guild, Warde compared type to a window "between the reader inside the room and that landscape which is the author's work." Ornate type like a stained-glass window, however admired, Warde warned, cannot provide a clear view of that landscape, and in fact obscures it. For Warde the beauty of type was not to be found in flourishes & curves, metered stress of slants & horizontals or in calculated geometric proportions but rather in their inconspicuousness. The subdued elegance of Verdana, sans serif except to distinguish characters, designed specifically for legibility—on the computer screen (that literal glass now virtually ubiquitous between the reader and world), yet pleasing on the printed page, would have charmed Ms. Warde.

Verdana was commissioned by Microsoft Corporation in the 1990s and developed by British type designer Matthew Carter. Before Carter designed Verdana for Microsoft in 1993, most computer typefaces had been adapted from traditional metal-set print type, often resulting in letters that appeared scrawny and pathetic (especially italics) on the low-resolution screens of the period. Virginia Howlett, then a member of Microsoft's typography team, recognized the demand for legible screen fonts and the prevailing popularity of contemporary sans-serif typefaces used in advertising like Helvetica and Univers. Matthew Carter was commissioned to collaborate on what remains to this day to be one of the most prevalent and popular of all computer fonts.

Dubbed "the most widely read man" (*The New Yorker*, 2005) for the volumes of text rendered in his still ever so popular type fonts (Verdana, Georgia, Tahoma, etc.), Carter has designed fonts for *Le Monde*, *The New York Times*, *Time*, *The Washington Post*, *The Boston Globe*, *Wired*, *Newsweek*, and *Sports Illustrated*, as well as Bell Centennial (commissioned by AT&T) for the phone book. In addition to commissions, his typography has earned him worldwide recognition and several awards including a MacArthur "genius grant" (2010). Seven of Carter's typefaces including

Verdana are in the permanent collection of the Museum of Modern Art, where they were displayed in MoMA's *Standard Deviations* exhibition (2011–12).

In 2009, the world's largest furniture retailer IKEA, famous for its savvy-marketing of design to the masses, caused a furor in the design and advertising communities by going *digital*—abandoning New Frankfurt's Futura to adopt Microsoft's Verdana for the design store's catalog typeface. While spokespeople for IKEA explained the change as a necessary step to unify branding between print and web media (Futura still proprietary and Verdana a widely distributed system font), critics were outraged that a typeface designed by Silicon Valley, specifically for the web, would supplant one by Werkbund, for books and as art, by appearing in print in the nearly 200 million catalogs distributed worldwide annually. However, the customers never complained.

Verdana was Brant Lyon's choice for the original 2006 saddle-stitched chapbook edition of *Your Infidel Eyes*. He said he wanted a sans-serif font, but no "geeky" Arial, nothing as "slick" as Helvetica, something more "humanist." He may have been secretly anticipating a future e-book, but his choice works quite well on paper. Like Lyon's writing, Verdana never obscures the landscape, and its calligraphic style well suits the human inhabitants. Proprietor of a cyber café outside Cairo (and not too far from the local IKEA), Brant would be delighted we (like IKEA) seconded his design choice of Verdana—on bright white paper—for the second, expanded, mass market edition of his—and Poets Wear Prada's—debut collection.